YOUR KNOWLEDGE HAS VALUE

- We will publish your bachelor's and master's thesis, essays and papers

- Your own eBook and book - sold worldwide in all relevant shops

- Earn money with each sale

Upload your text at www.GRIN.com and publish for free

Mohamed Rhounan

The American Dream and its role in the Declaration of Independence

GRIN Verlag

Bibliografische Information der Deutschen Nationalbibliothek:

Die Deutsche Bibliothek verzeichnet diese Publikation in der Deutschen National-
bibliografie; detaillierte bibliografische Daten sind im Internet über http://dnb.d-
nb.de/ abrufbar.

Imprint:

Copyright © 2013 GRIN Verlag GmbH
Druck und Bindung: Books on Demand GmbH, Norderstedt Germany
ISBN: 978-3-656-57502-3

This book at GRIN:

http://www.grin.com/en/e-book/264058/the-american-dream-and-its-role-in-the-
declaration-of-independence

GRIN - Your knowledge has value

Der GRIN Verlag publiziert seit 1998 wissenschaftliche Arbeiten von Studenten, Hochschullehrern und anderen Akademikern als eBook und gedrucktes Buch. Die Verlagswebsite www.grin.com ist die ideale Plattform zur Veröffentlichung von Hausarbeiten, Abschlussarbeiten, wissenschaftlichen Aufsätzen, Dissertationen und Fachbüchern.

Visit us on the internet:

http://www.grin.com/

http://www.facebook.com/grincom

http://www.twitter.com/grin_com

The American Dream and its role in the
Declaration of Independence

Content

1. Introduction

The American Dream is one of the most famous ethos in the world. Many people believed and still believe in this ethos which is a set of ideals in which the meaning of freedom is connected to the opportunity for prosperity and succes. An upward social mobility is accieved by hard work and dedication. The idea of the American Dream has is origin in the United States Declaration of Independence which was written by Thomas Jefferson in 1776. Terms like "The Pursuit of Happiness", "all men are created equal" are considered as important human rights. The pursuit of happines is closely related to the idea of the American Dream. It belongs to the inalienable rights which cannot be denied. Every American has the right to realize his individuel dreams without beeing stopped.

But what is actually meant by the this term? What is the American Dream and how important is it fort the American society? In the following I will deal with different aspects of the American Dream and take a closer look at this idea in order determine its signifi- cance for the American society.

Caricature of the American Dream[1]

---

[1]http://chabelyvalera.files.wordpress.com/2013/01/20081123_barack_obama_co mic_01.gif (31/10/2013) 12:01

2. Meaning of the American Dream

A clear definition of the American Dream does not exist. Every American citizen has his own idea of the American Dream in mind. For some people the American Dream is related to property and high living standards and for other people it is related to the pursuing of happiness like it is mentioned in the Declaration of Independence. Still we dont know exactly what Jefferson wanted to express by using this term: "No one knows precisely what Jefferson had in mind when he asserted "the pursuit of happiness" as one of mankind's unalienable rights. The phrase is in some measure a substitution for Locke's "property", but most historians agree that Jefferson intended something more inclusive and dynmaic both."[2] As we can see there is indeed something revolutionary what Jefferson had in mind. The "Pursuit of Happiness" is a new social idea that breaks all old-fashioned social conventions and creates new opportunities: "According to the most recent student of the Declaration of Independence, "When Jefferson spoke of pursuing happiness, he had nothing vague or private in mind. He meant a public happiness which is measurable...."[3] The American Dream is basicly a dream of a good life. By following this idea the American citizen tries to improve his life and to fulfill his dreams. By mentioning it in the Declaration of Idependence Jefferson wanted to gurantee this right to all American citizens no matter from where they come from so that the USA can be considered as a nation of endless posibilities.

At the end of the 18th century with the foundation of the US millions of people immigrated to the US in order to escape from political problems and to build up a new life: "Principles, hope, and liberty were powerful attractions, and would remain so for subsequent generations who came here from all over the world."[4] The US was seen as a new chance to live in freedom and to realize the own ideas which was not posible at that time in Europe. Because of the great variety of people we cannot see the idea of the American Dream as one single idea but more as a set of different individual ideas which belong to different persons.

---

[2] Lewis, Jan (1983): *The pursuit of happiness*, New York: Press Syndicate of the University of Cambridge. P. 8
[3] Ebd.
[4] Cullen, Jim (2003): *The American Dream*, Oxfod: Oxford University Press. P.17

3. The nation and its relation to the American Dream

"[...] that American dream of a better, richer, and happier life for all our citizens of every rank, which is the greatest contribution we have made to the thought and welfare of the world. That dream or hope has been present from the start. Ever since we became an indepedent nation, each generation has seen an uprising of ordinary Americans to save that dream from the forces which appeared to be overhelming it."[5]

As we can see the idea of the American Dream is hardly related to the nation. It has become an important component of the American nation and identity: "The term seems like the most lofty as well as the most immediate component of an American identity, a birthright far more meaningful and compelling than terms like "democracy", "Constitution," or even "the United States.""[6]

Ever since the American Dream is something untouchable that cannot be definied exactly. It is indeed as we saw before strongly related to the nation because it was considered like a source of power for the people that build up the nation: "The American Dream would have no drama or mystique if it were a self-evident falsehood or a scientifically demonstrable principle. Ambiguity is the very source of its mystic power, nowhere more so than among those striving for, but unsure whether they will reach, their goals."[7] The uncertainty about the idea of the American Dream is an essential factor that keeps it alive. Through this fact we can explain us easily the existence of the varieties of the American Dream: "The answers vary. Sometimes "better and richer and fuller" is defined in terms of money – in the contemporary United States, one could almost believe this is the *only* definition – but there are others. Religious transformation, political reform, educational attainment, sexual expression: the list is endless."[8] All in all we can say that there is a strong relation between the American nation and the idea of the American Dream that is considered as an key element of the American identity.

---

[5] Cullen, Jim (2003): *The American Dream*, Oxfod: Oxford University Press. P. 4
[6] Ebd.
[7] Ebd.
[8] Ebd. P. 7

4.   The Declaration of Independence

The Declaration of Independence is a political manifesto that can be seen as the charter of the American Dream. It was the trigger of the American Revolution against the British. This document includes several rights and ideas written down by Thomas Jefferson. His aim was it to form a stabil and independent nation: "Thomas Jefferson's achievement in 1776 was to use his forensic and rhetorical skill to forge an instrument for declaring independence without any earlier models to guide him."[9] In this set of rights and ideas there is mentioned the Pursuit of Happiness which is related to the American Dream: "The Declaration spoke both of the righst of free and independent states and of the rights of "all Men" to "Life, Liberty, and the Pursuit of Happiness."[10] The Declaration of Independence has not only given rights to America, it was more like an role model for many other countries: "[...] the Declaration set forth a philosophy of human rights that could be apllied not only to Americans but to peoples everywhere. It was essential in giving the American Revolution a universal appeal."[11]

5.   Conclusion

The aim of this work was it to take a closer look at the idea of the American Dream and its relation to the Declaration of Independence. We have seen that this national ethos is hardly related to the American identity and culture. We cannot determine one single definition for it because it dependes on the great variety of people that strongly believe in this kind of dream. Although the American Dream is not something that we can describe easily it contains a set of principeles that one should follow to become what ever he wants to become. The hope of getting foreword and fulfilling his own dreams by dedication and hard work is a powerful atraction for millions of people not only in America but all over the world. This is exactly the place where the idea of the American Dream gets out its power. The Pursuit of Happiness is mentioned in the

---

[9] Armitage, David (2007): T*he Declaration of Independence*, London: Harvard University Press. P. 140
[10] Ebd.
[11] Ebd. P. 139

Declaration of Independence which means it is the right of everyone to search for his own happiness without beeing stopped. This is the main idea behind the American Dream. It offers to anybody who believes in it many possibilities to choose the own way in life. All in all the American dream has got a very significant role in the Declaration of Independence because it is the head of the main idea or furthermore the wish of a nation who wanted to realize itself and become independet.

6. Bibliography

Armitage, David (2007): T*he Declaration of Independence*, London: Harvard University Press.

Carter, Everett (1977): *The American Idea*, North Carolina: The University of North Carolina Press.

Cullen, Jim (2003): *The American Dream*, Oxfod: Oxford University Press.
Delbanco, Andrew (1999): *The real American Dream*, London: Harvard University Press.

H. Holbrook, Stewart (1957): Dreamers of the American Dream, New York: Doubleday & Company, Inc., Garden City.

Lewis, Jan (1983): *The pursuit of happiness*, New York: Press Syndicate of the University of Cambridge

Images:
Caricature of the American Dream:
http://chabelyvalera.files.wordpress.com/2013/01/20081123_barack_obama_comic_01.gif (31/10/2013) 12:01